THE LEGEND OF THE 12 ANIMALS

ILLUSTRATED BY PETER WONG

CONTENTS

STORY

The legend goes that the Jade Emperor ordered all the animals that inhabited the earth to congratulate him on his birthday on January 9th one year. He determined to select the 12 animals that arrived first to be guards of the Heavenly Gate, so they could take turns on duty in order to prevent deities from secretly descending to the earth.

All the animals were very excited and were itching to start upon hearing the good news. The Jade Emperor made a rule that all animals would run across a river, and each animal's position in the zodiac would be set by its place in the race.

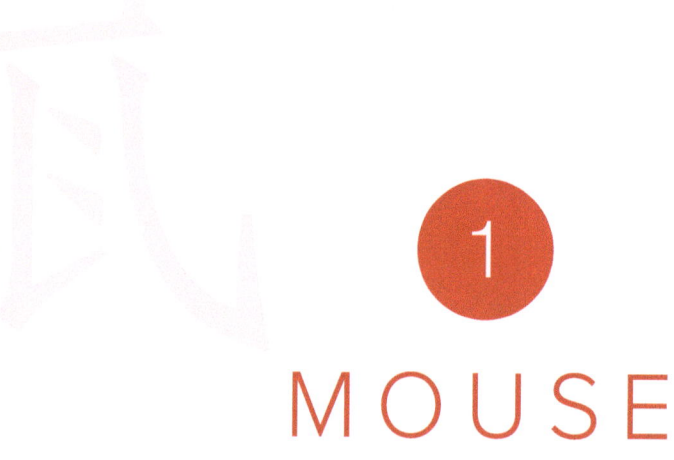

1

MOUSE
Jan 25 2020–Feb 11 2021

The witty mouse stopped by the river owing to the swift current. Having waited for a long time, clever mouse saw the ox crossing the river, so he swiftly jumped onto the ox's head.

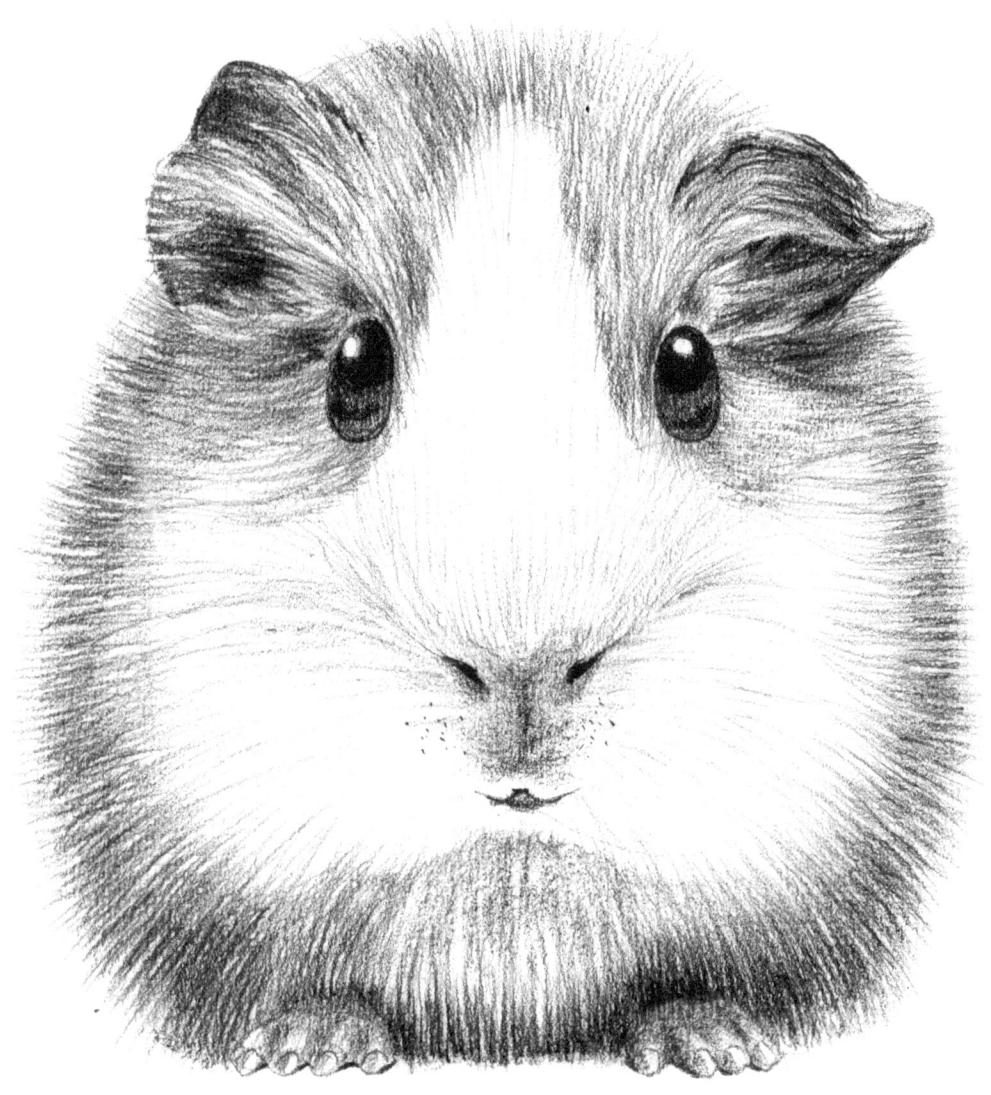

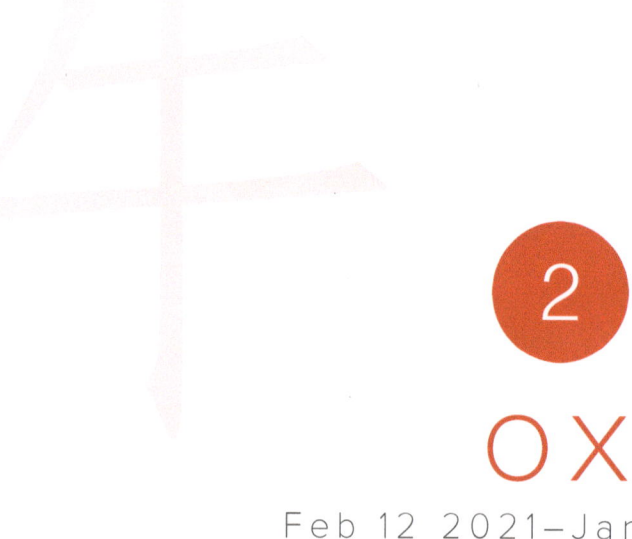

2

O X

Feb 12 2021–Jan 31 2022

The kindhearted ox did not mind at all to let the mouse sit on its head, so it kept on crossing the river. After crossing it, the mouse jumped down from ox's head and that made ox second place and mouse first place.

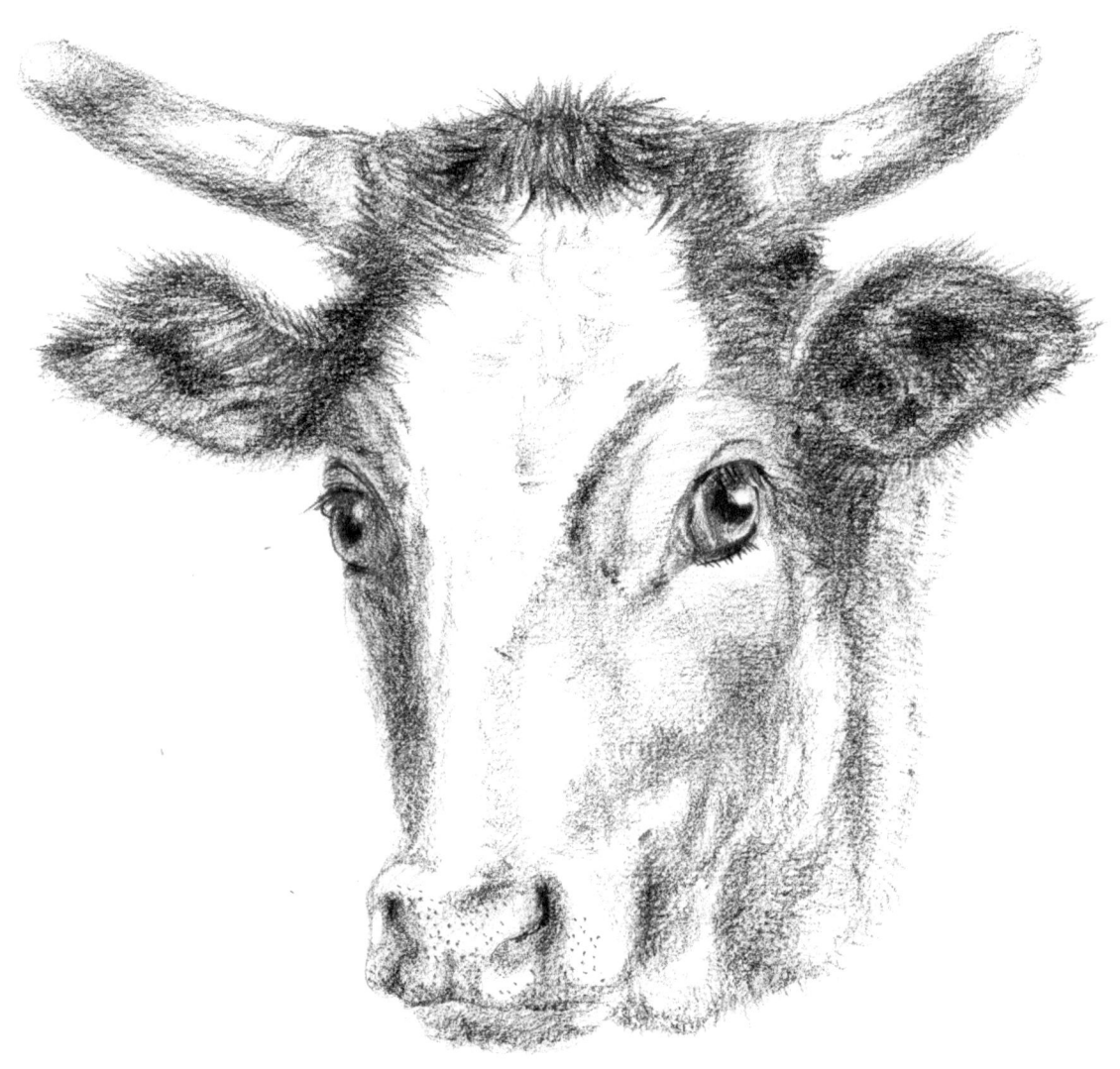

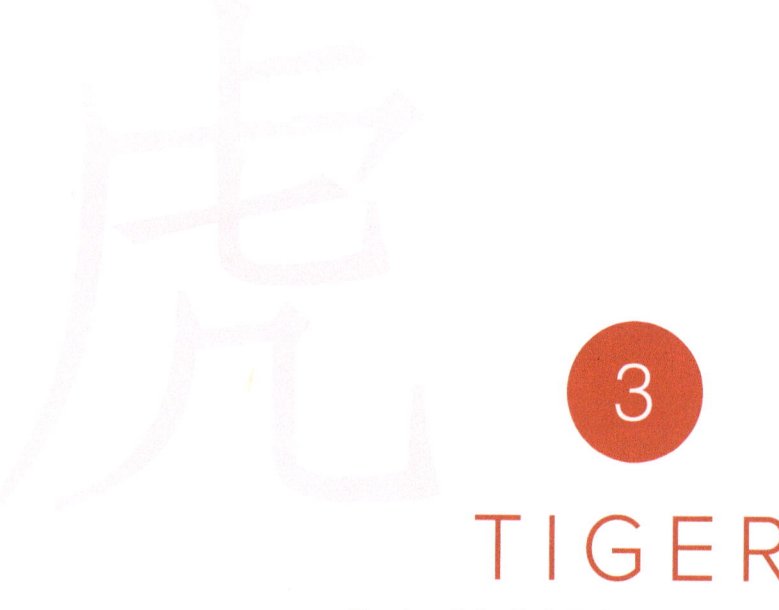

3

TIGER

Feb 01 2022–Jan 21 2023

The authoritative and courageous tiger jumped into the river with no fear or doubts. It swam as fast as it could and got third place.

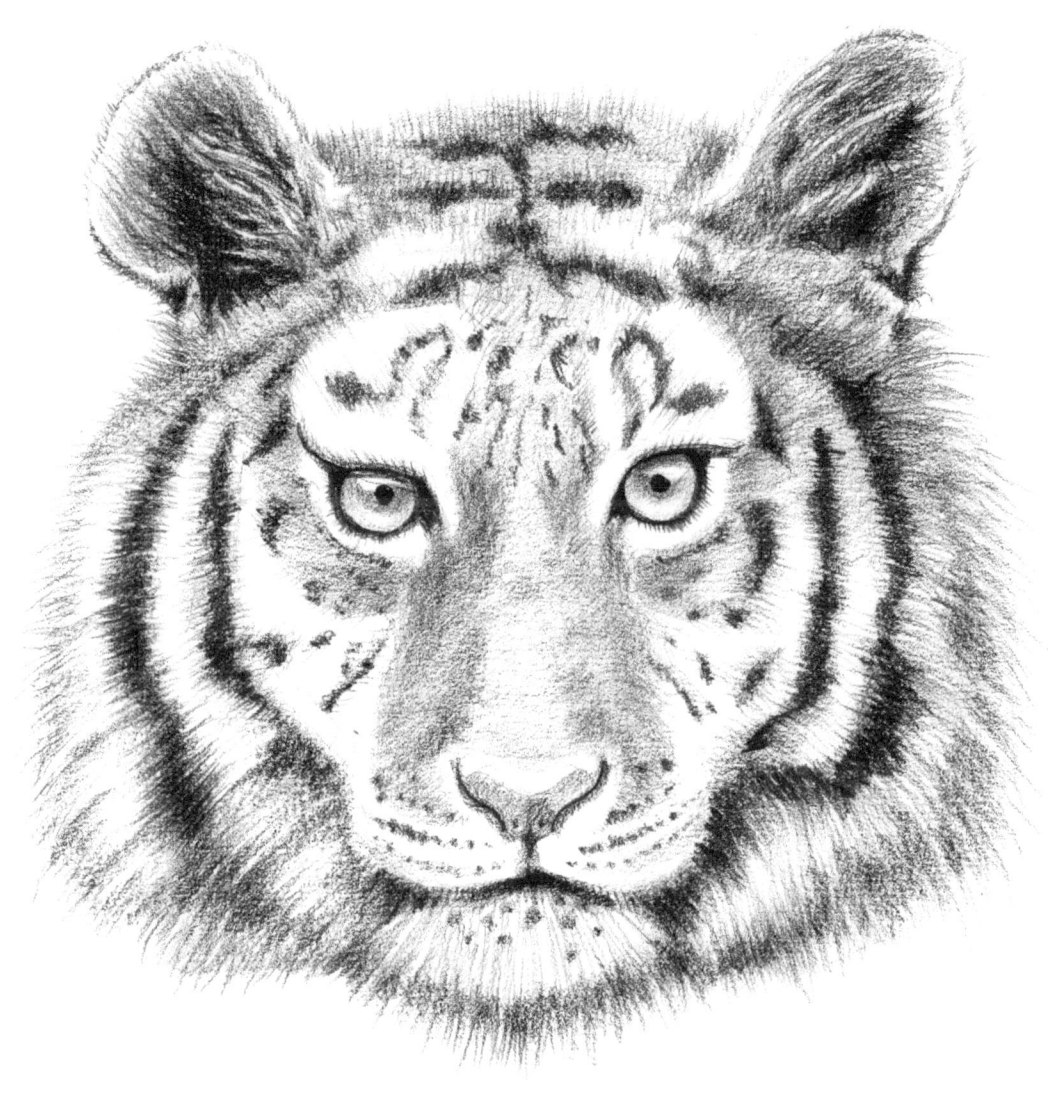

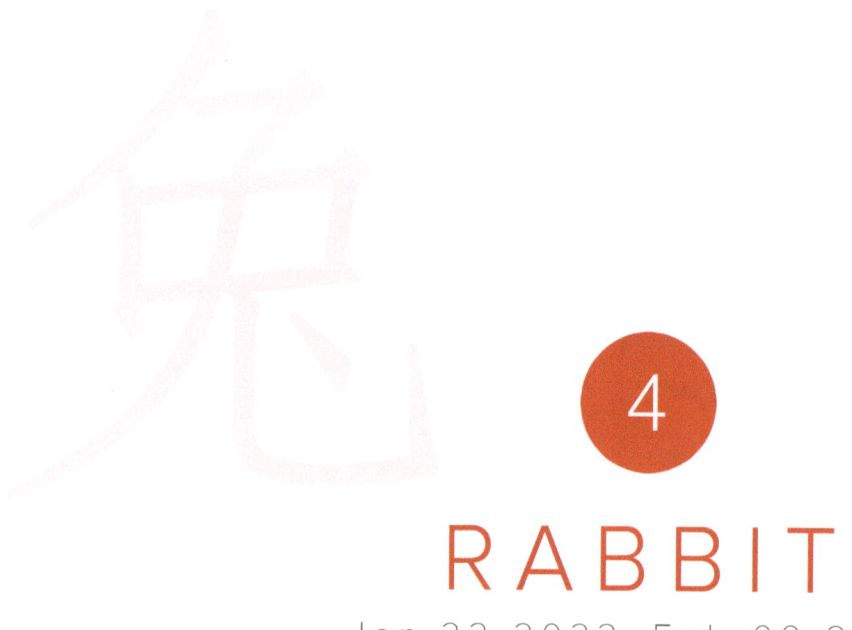

4

RABBIT

Jan 22 2023–Feb 09 2024

The quick and alert rabbit found a trail of logs in the river, and it quickly hopped on them to reach the finish line with fourth place.

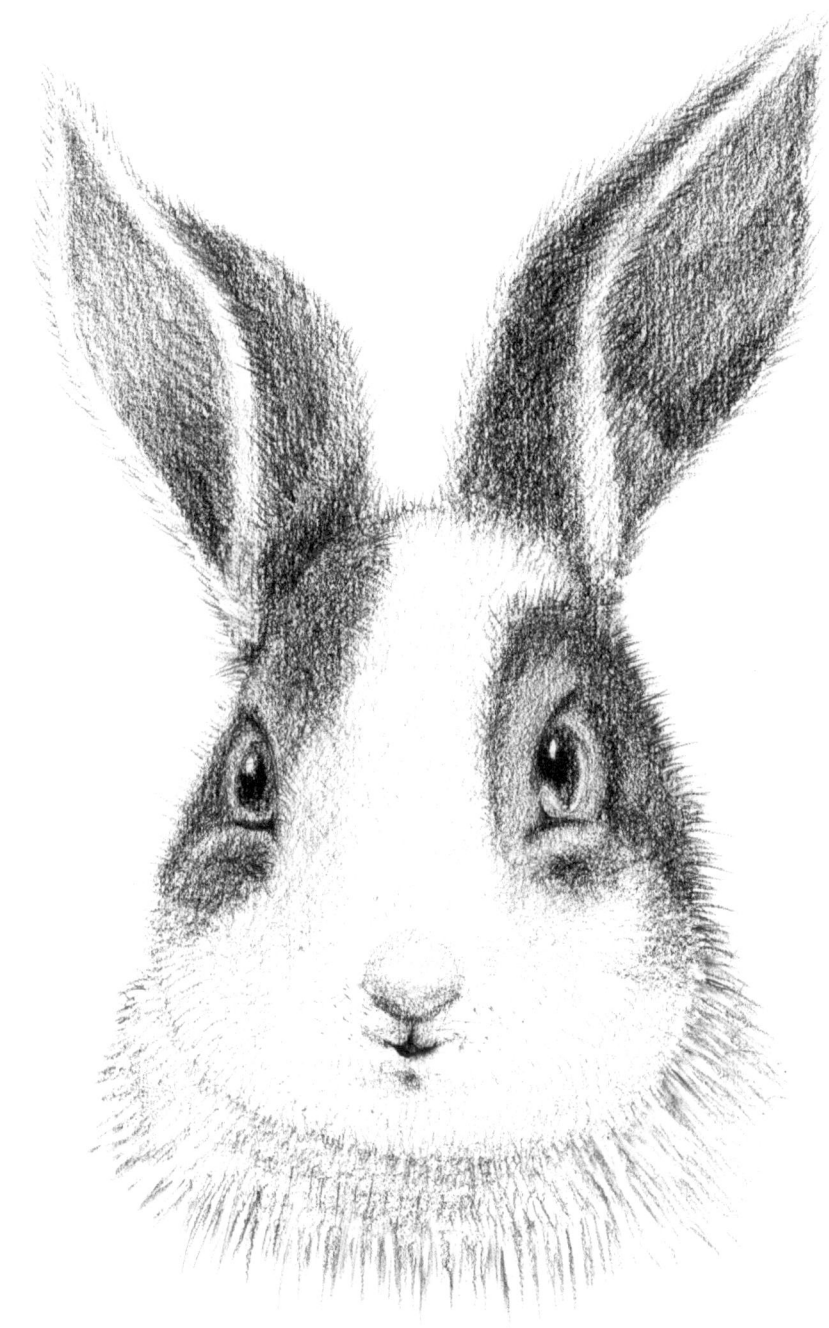

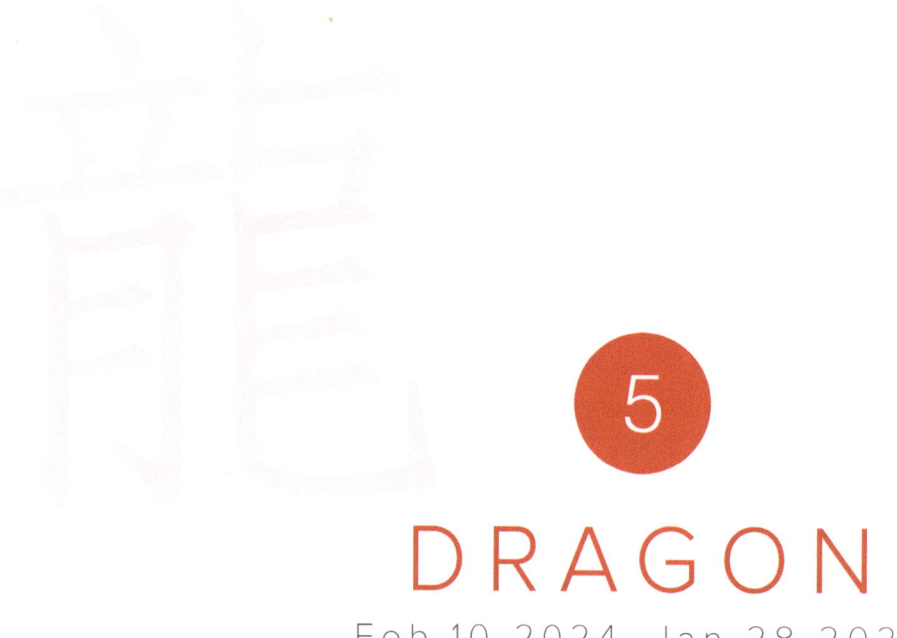

5

DRAGON

Feb 10 2024—Jan 28 2025

The powerful and mystical dragon had the favor to win the race, since he can fly. But along the race, he stopped by the village to help make rain to stop a fire. The kindhearted dragon finished the race with fifth place.

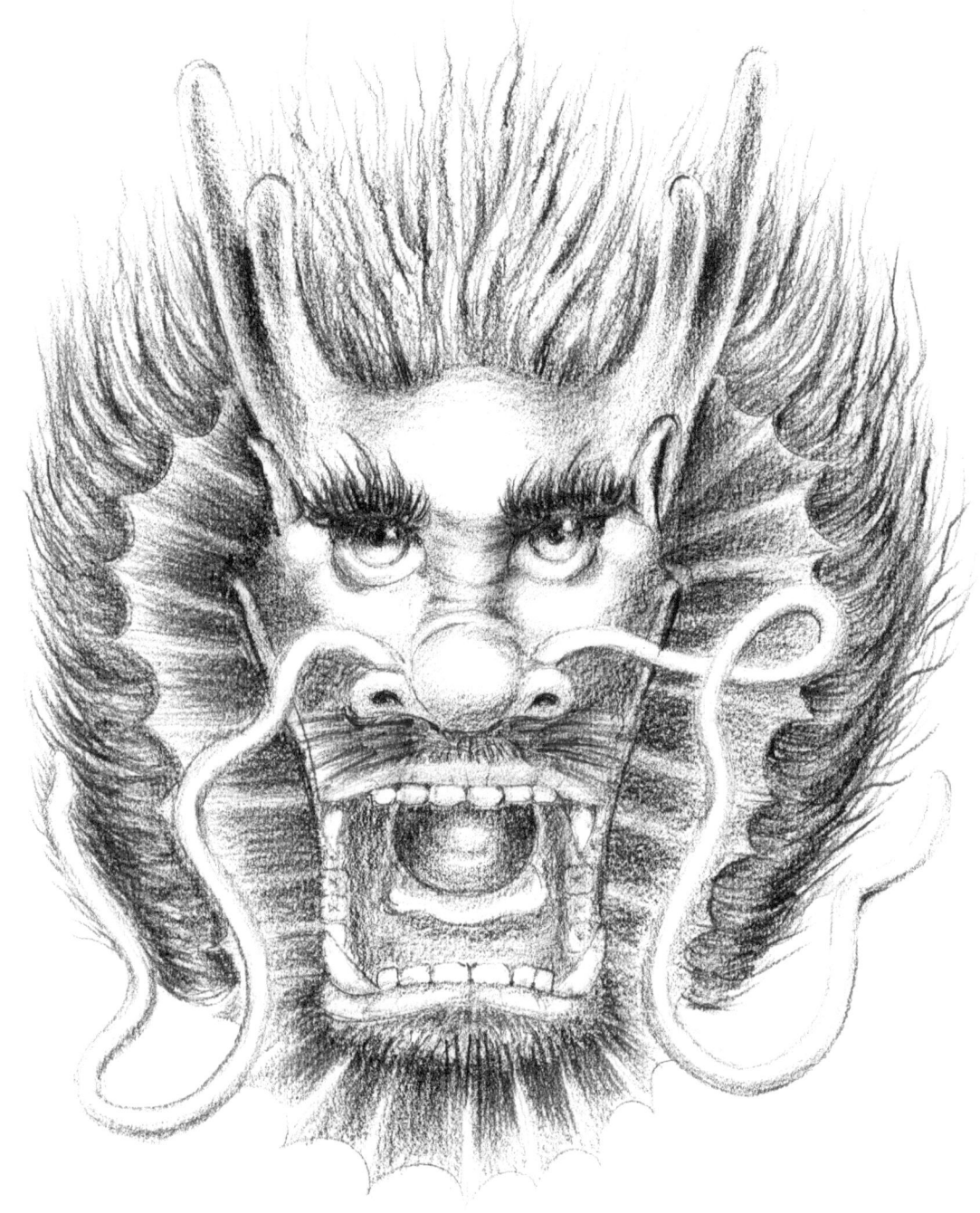

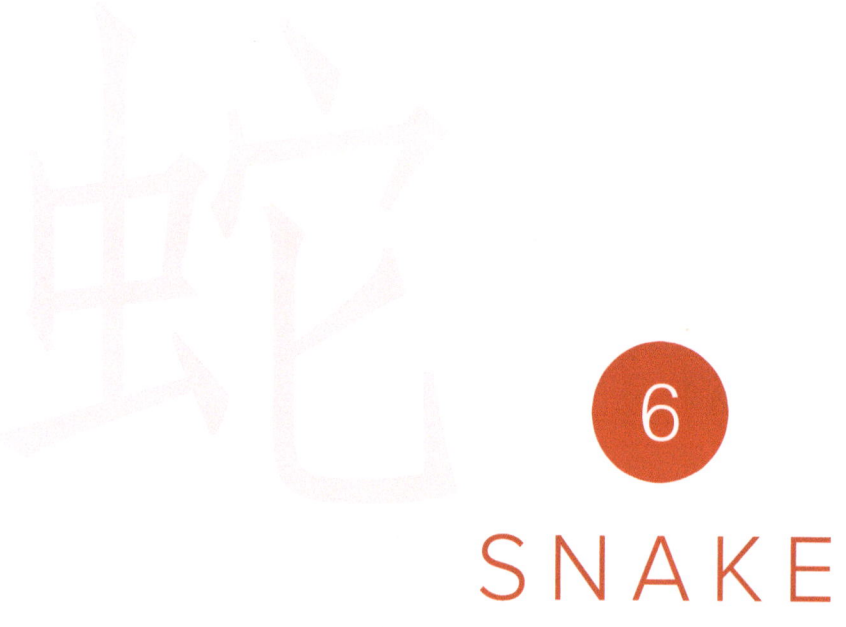

6

SNAKE

Jan 29 2025–Feb 16 2026

The charming and smart snake securely hitched a ride on the horse's leg and the snake slithered across the finish line with sixth place.

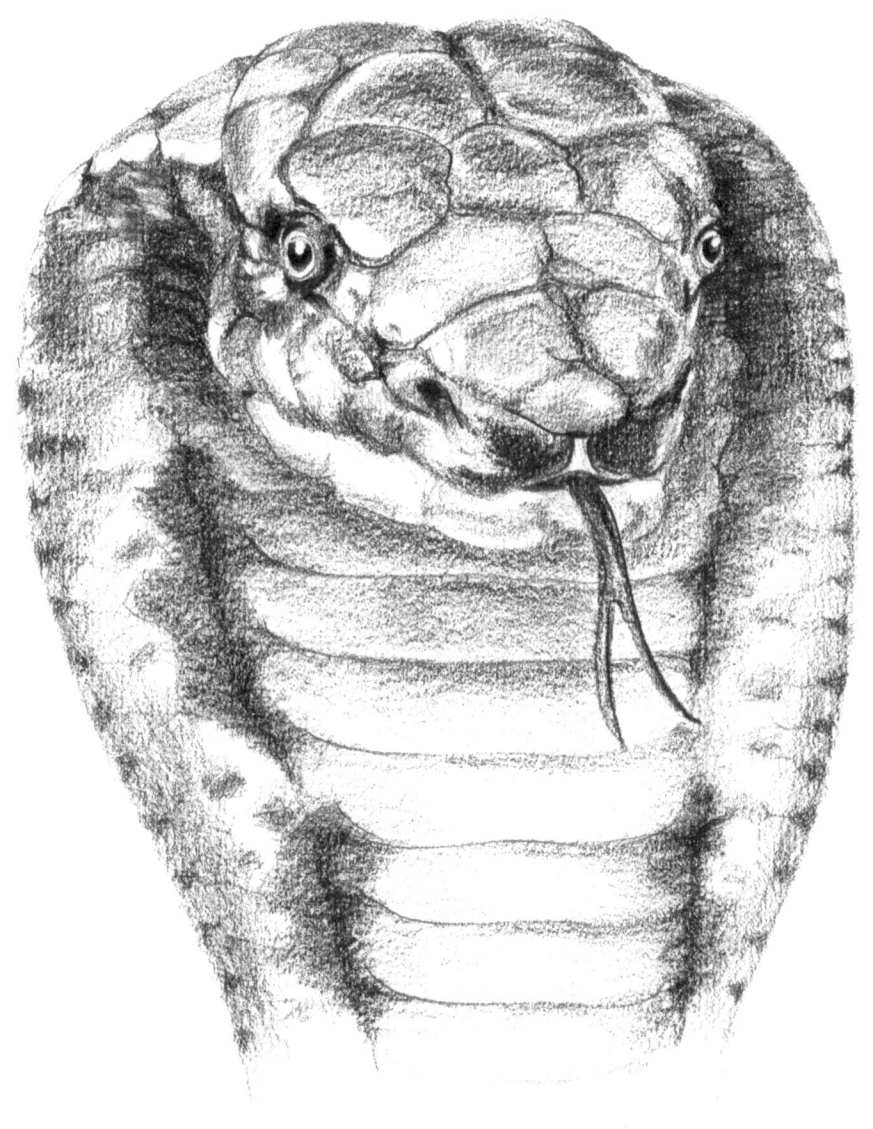

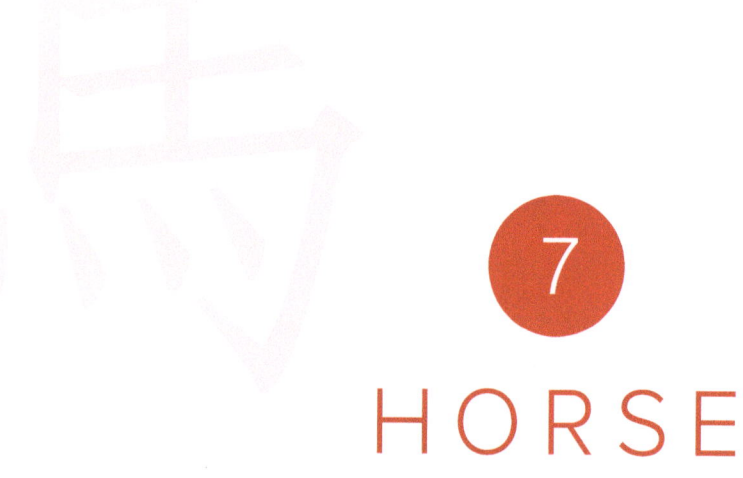

7

HORSE

Feb 17 2026–Feb 05 2027

The strong and elegant horse swam across the river like a wind and finished the race with a close seventh place.

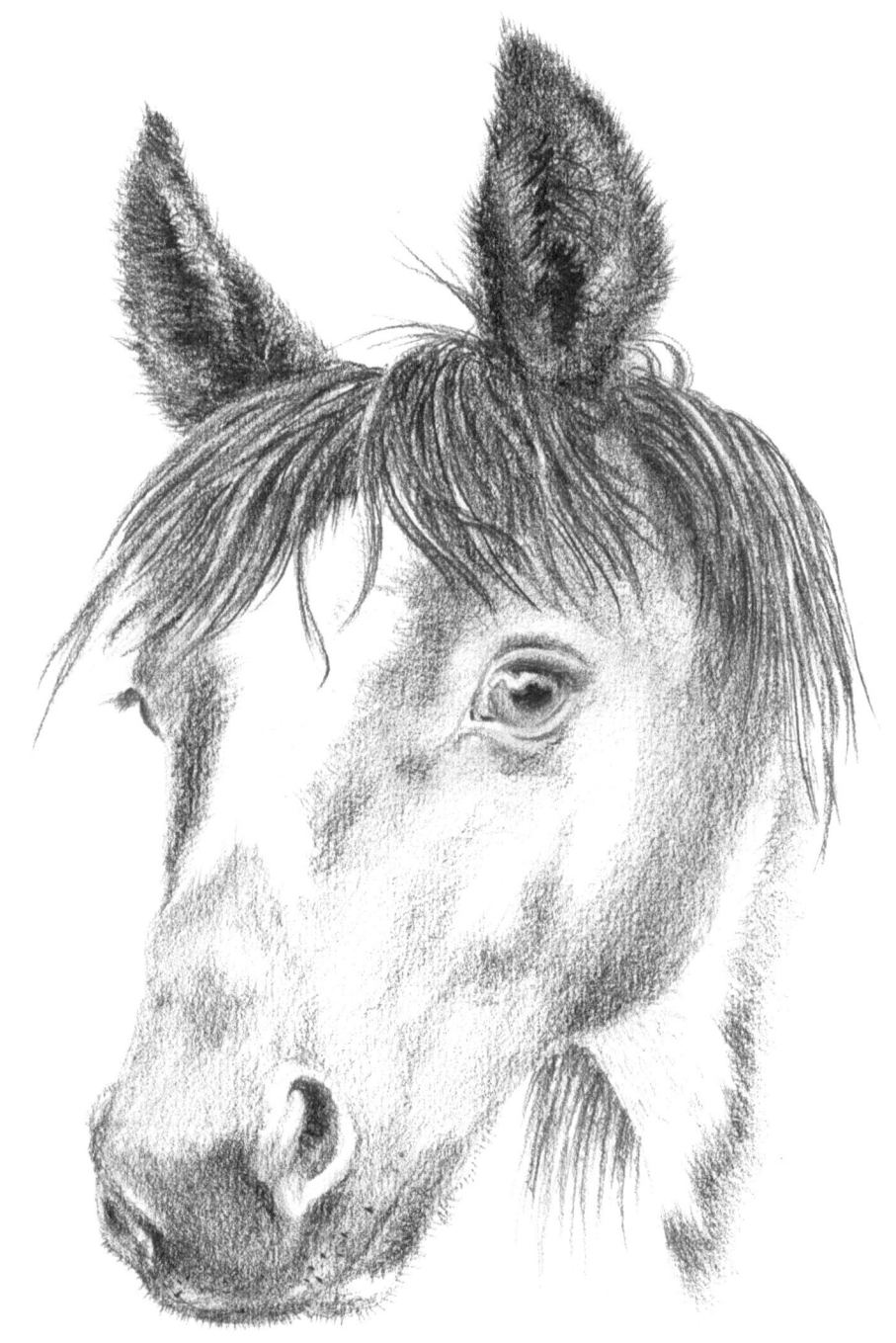

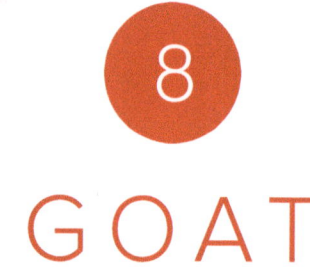

GOAT

Feb 17 2027–Feb 05 2028

The kind and peace-loving goat teamed up with the monkey and rooster to cross the river. They spotted a raft and with a lot of pulling and paddling, they all reached the finish line. The Jade Emperor was pleased with their teamwork, and honored the goat with eighth place.

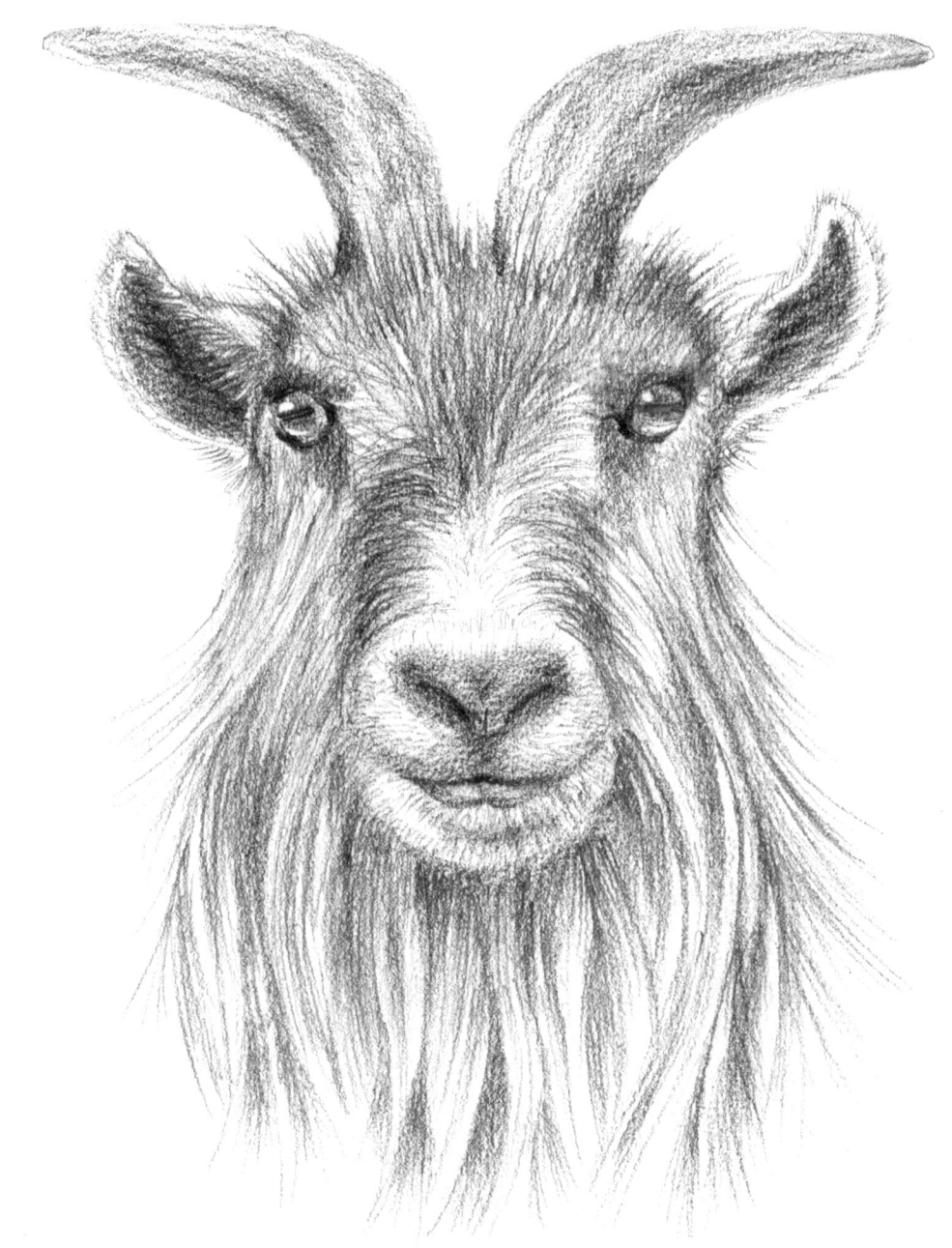

9

MONKEY

Feb 17 2028–Feb 05 2029

The playful and energetic monkey was grateful to have teamed up with the goat and rooster to cross the river. The Jade Emperor was impressed with monkey's teamwork and honored the monkey with ninth place.

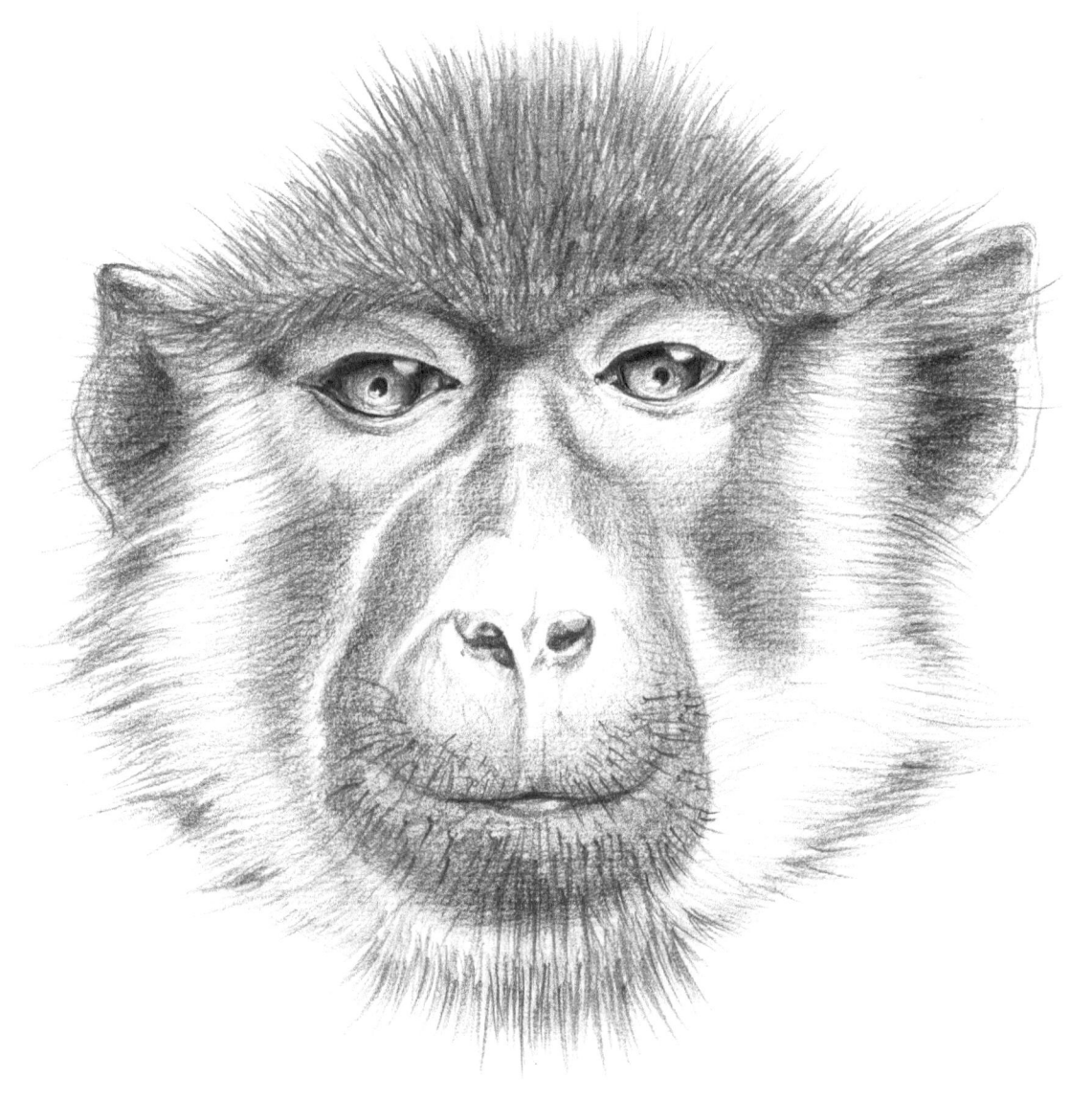

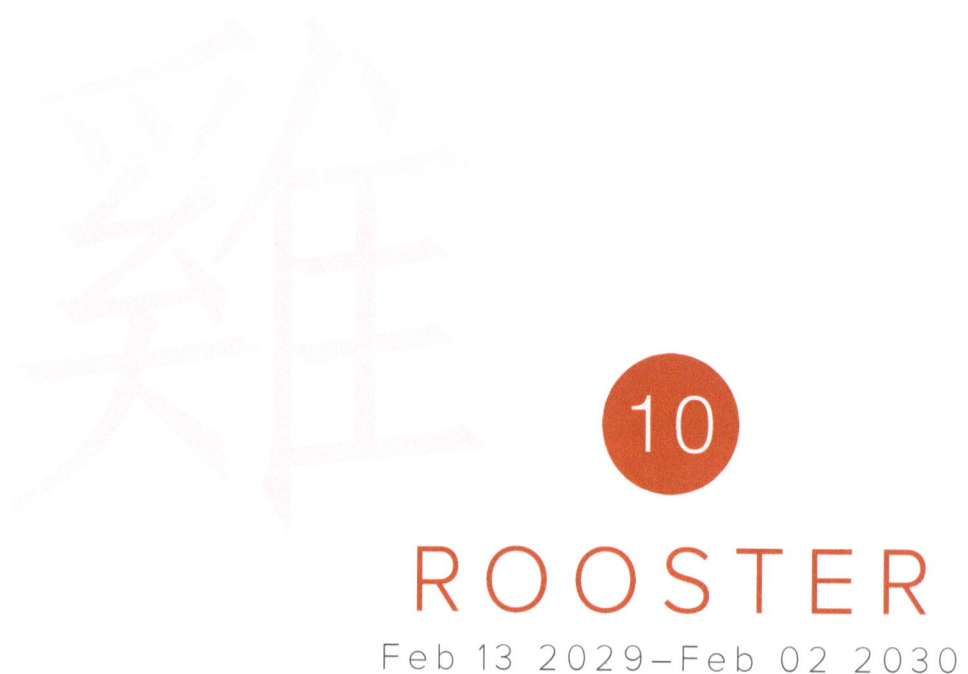

10

ROOSTER

Feb 13 2029–Feb 02 2030

The hard-working and observant rooster was thankful to have teamed up with the goat and monkey since it doesn't know how to swam. The Jade Emperor was happy with rooster's teamwork and honored the rooster with tenth place.

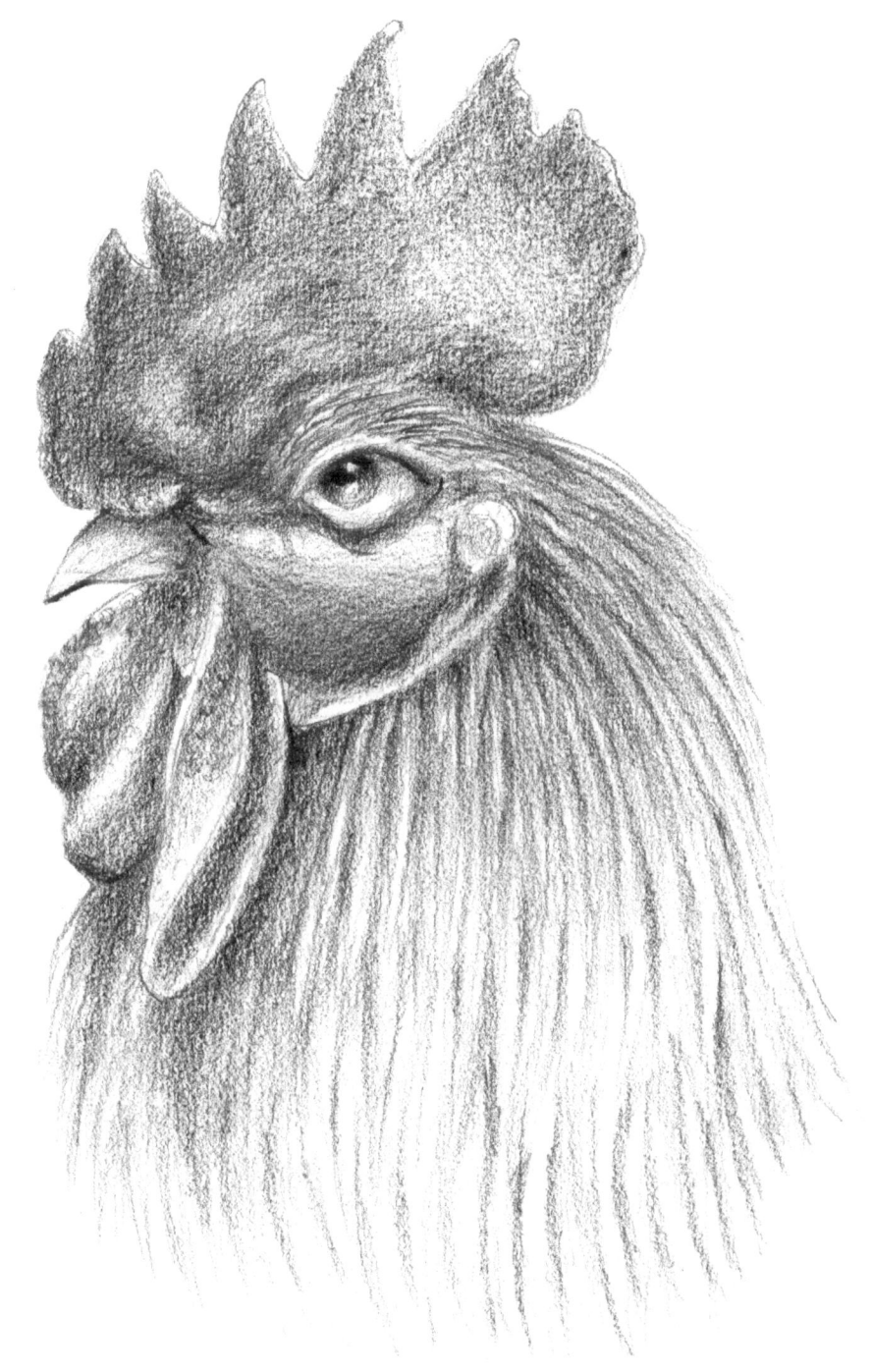

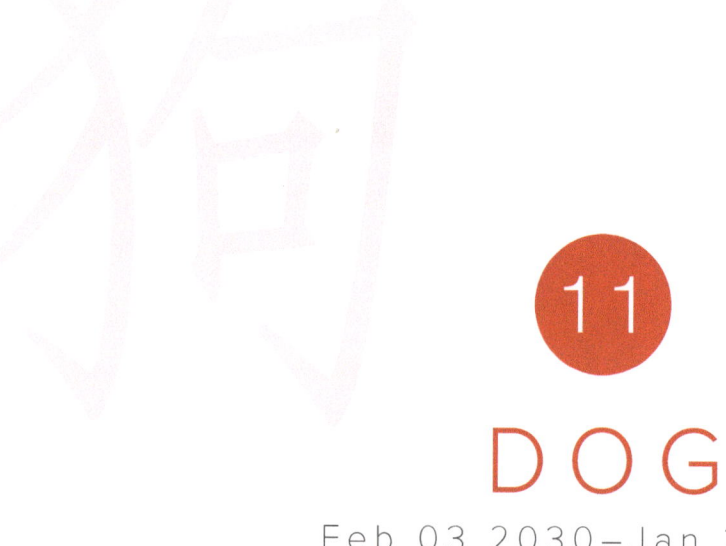

11

DOG

Feb 03 2030–Jan 22 2031

The diligent and patient dog enjoyed the cool river as it paddled across the river. But, it managed to finish the race with eleventh place.

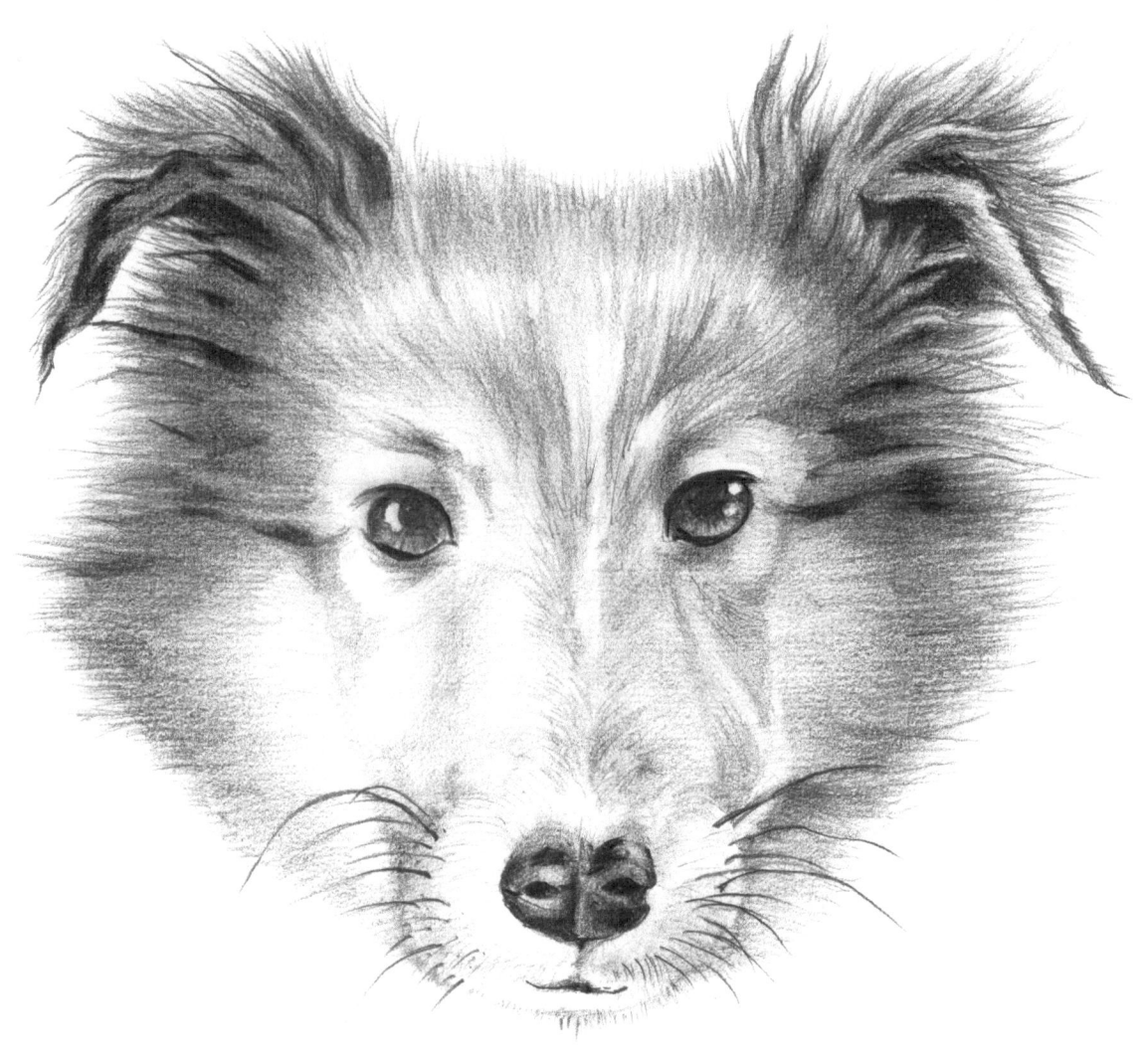

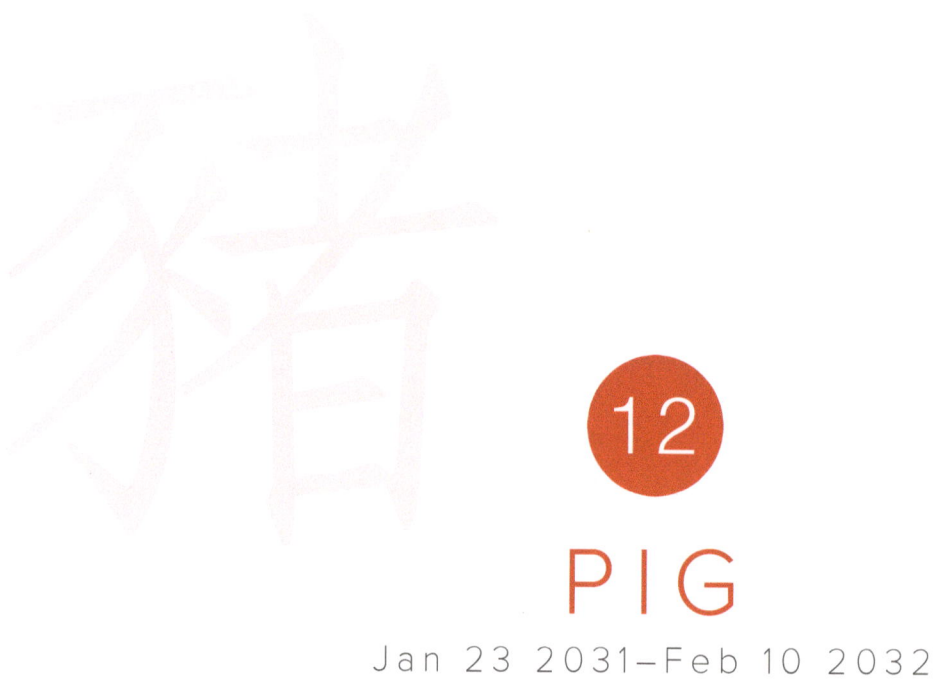

PIG

Jan 23 2031–Feb 10 2032

The loving and honest pig took a nap along the race, but with its smart sense it still managed get to the finish line. Even though pig got last place, it still held a positive spirit to celebrate Jade Emperor's birthday.

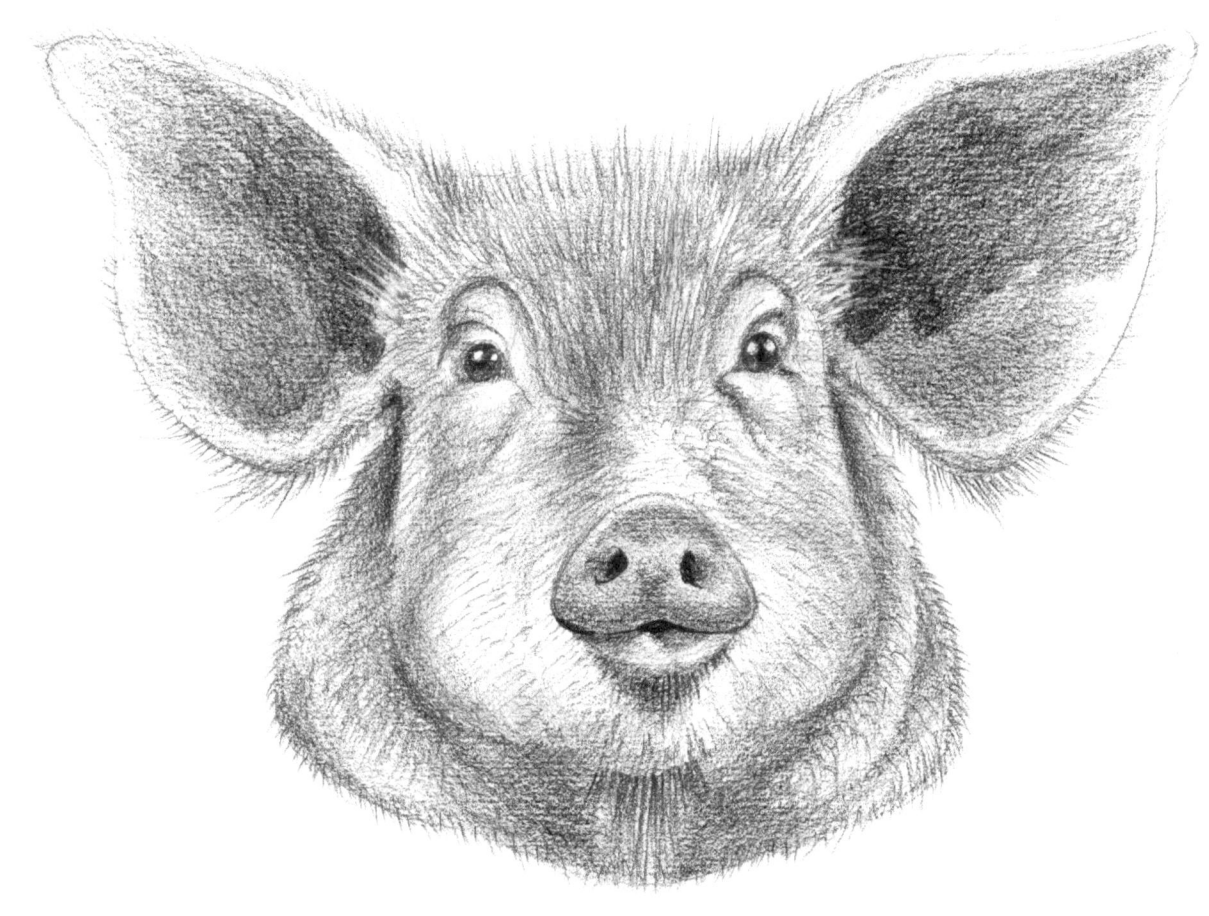

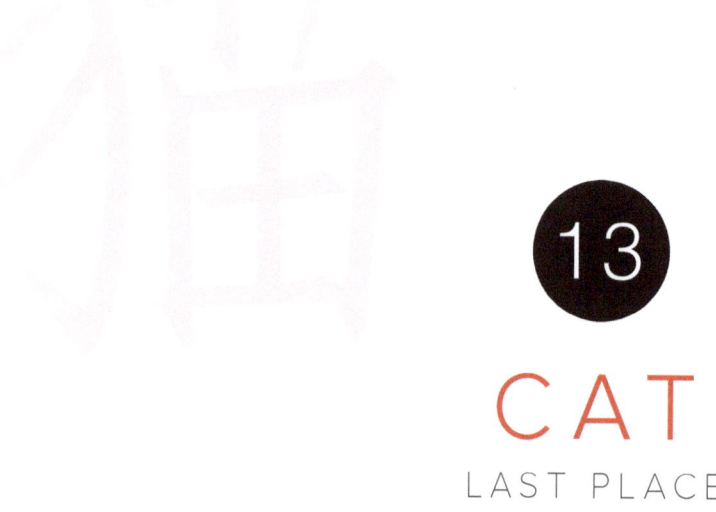

13

CAT

LAST PLACE

When it came time to leave, however, the cat was taking a nap. The mouse, realizing that he would have to use all his cunning to be noticed by the Jade Emperor, left his friend sleeping, and set off on his own. This is why there is no year named after the cat, and also why cats have hated mice ever since.

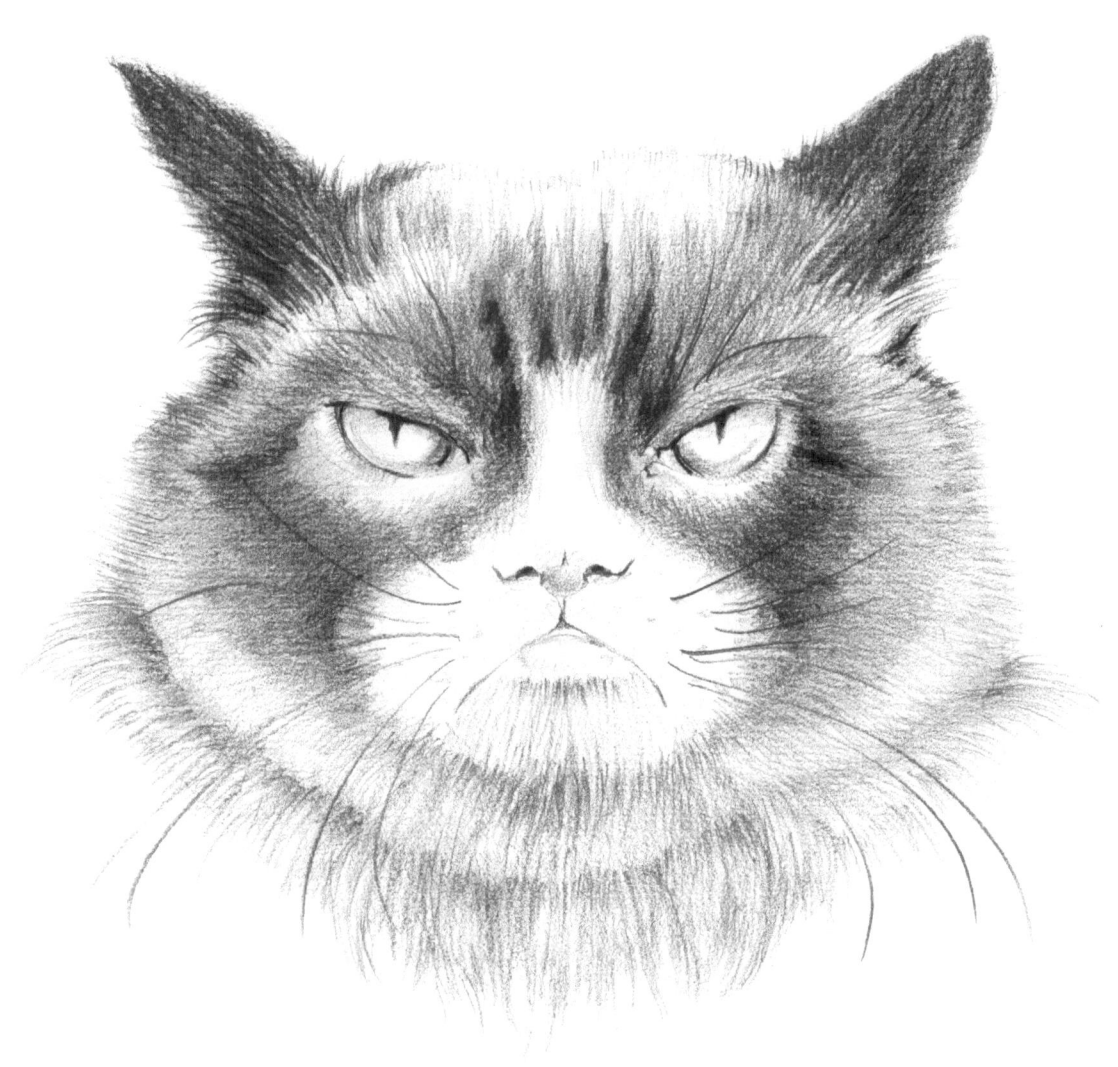

MAY YOUR YEAR BE FILLED WITH BLESSINGS.